W9-DCJ-310

Finding a Way

Six Historic U.S. Routes

by Anastasia Suen

PRAIRIE VIEW ELEMENTARY
1730 REGENT ST.
GOSHEN, IN 46526

CELEBRATION PRESS
Pearson Learning Group

The following people from **Pearson Learning Group**
have contributed to the development of this product:

Leslie Beierstone-Barna, Cindy Kane **Editorial**
Tricia Battipede, Joan Mazzeo, Janice Noto-Helmers **Design**
Salita Mehta **Photo Research**
Dan Trush **Art Buying**
Content Area Consultant Dr. Linda Greenow

Marketing Christine Fleming
Publishing Operations Jennifer Van Der Heide
Production/Manufacturing Laura Benford-Sullivan,
Susan Levine, Michele Uhl

The following people from **DK** have
contributed to the development of this program:

Art Director Rachael Foster
Scarlett O'Hara **Managing Editor** | **Editor UK Editions** Marie Greenwood

Photo Credits: All photographs are by David Mager, Elbaliz Mendez, and Judy Mahoney
of the Pearson Learning Group Photo Studio except as noted below.
All photography © Pearson Education, Inc. (PEI) unless otherwise specifically noted.

Front Cover: *bkgd.* © George H.H. Huey/Corbis; *frgd.* © Bettmann/Corbis. 1: Andre Jenny/Focus Group/PictureQuest. 4: © Bettmann/Corbis.
5: © Library of Congress, Washington DC/SuperStock. 6–7: Eileen Tweedy/The Picture Desk/The Art Archive/Kobal. 7: Hulton Archive/Getty Images,
Inc. 8: *t.* U.S. Department of Transportation Federal Highway Administration; *b.* © Tecmap Corporation/Eric Curry/Corbis.
9: Alex MacLean/Landslides. 10: Thomas Brummett/Hulton Archive/Getty Images, Inc. 11: © Bettmann/Corbis. 12: *t.* Missouri Historical Society;
b. Mark Twain Memorial. 13: © Annie Griffiths Belt/Corbis. 14: © Kennan Ward/Corbis. 15: © Richard A. Cooke/Corbis. 16: *t.* U.S. Department
of Commerce; *b.* U.S. Department of Transportation Federal Highway Administration. 17: National Society, Daughters of the American Revolution.
18: Florence Griswold Musuem, Old Lyme, Connecticut, USA/Bridgeman Art Library. Gift of the Hartford Steam Boiler Inspection & Insurance Co.
19: New York Historical Society, New York, NY/The Bridgeman Art Library. 20: Andre Jenny/Focus Group/PictureQuest. 21: *t.* © Bettmann/Corbis;
b. Rochester Images: From the Rochester City Hall Photo Lab. 23: The Granger Collection. 24: © James L. Amos/Corbis. 25: *t.* From the Collection
of the Clackamas County Historical Society, Museum of the Oregon Territory; *b.* Wyoming Recreation Commission. 26: The Granger Collection.
27: © Corbis. 28: Huntington Library/SuperStock, Inc. 29: *t.* George H.H. Huey/George H.H. Huey Photography, Inc.; *b.* The Granger Collection.
30: Courtesy, Anastasia Suen.
Illustrations: Border: Joel Iskowitz. 7, 10, 17, 20, 22, Back Cover: XNR Productions. 14, 15: Kenneth Batelman. 19, 24, 28, 29: Dan Trush.

Text Copyright © 2005 Pearson Education, Inc., publishing as Celebration Press, a division of Pearson Learning Group. Compilation
Copyright © 2005 Dorling Kindersley Ltd. All rights reserved. No part of this book may be reproduced or transmitted in any form
or by any means, electronic or mechanical, including photocopying, recording, or any information storage and retrieval system,
without permission in writing from the proprietors.

For information regarding licensing and permissions, write to Rights and Permissions Department, Pearson Learning Group,
299 Jefferson Road, Parsippany, NJ 07054 USA or to Rights and Permissions Department, DK Publishing,
The Penguin Group (UK), 80 Strand, London WC2R 0RL.

Lexile is a U.S. registered trademark of MetaMetrics, Inc. All right reserved.

ISBN: 0-7652-5239-2

Color reproduction by Colourscan, Singapore
Printed in the United States of America
6 7 8 9 10   08 07

1-800-321-3106
www.pearsonlearning.com

Contents

Introduction   4

The Boston Post Road   6

The Mighty Mississippi   10

The National Road   14

The Erie Canal   18

The Oregon Trail   22

The Transcontinental Railroad   26

Conclusion   30

Glossary   31

Index   32

Introduction

The first people to live in what is now America arrived on foot. Thousands of years ago, people from Asia crossed a land bridge to reach North America. This strip of land connected what is now Siberia to Alaska. Moving from west to east, the travelers settled all across the **continent**. The land bridge disappeared in time, covered by ocean water.

Centuries later, European explorers and traders arrived in the Americas by ship. Maps were made of "The New World." It was a mapmaker who named the continent of South America after the Italian explorer Amerigo Vespucci. The name was later used for North America as well.

Italian explorer Amerigo Vespucci

This map of *Die Nüw Welt* (The New World) was published in 1550.

4

People have always been on the move in the country that is now called the United States of America. Native American peoples, the first Americans, used footpaths to travel from one place to another. Often these paths were trails that had been made by animals. Most were only wide enough for a single person. Over time, these routes were widened to allow for horses, wagons, and eventually cars. In the course of several centuries, a trail through the forest might become a six-lane highway.

Native Americans also used waterways for travel, just as people have done in cultures around the globe since ancient times. These water routes were also altered as time passed.

Routes have always changed and developed as people's needs changed. This book looks at six historic U.S. routes and explores why and how they came to be.

Native Americans used both trails and waterways for travel.

The Boston Post Road

In early colonial America, mail sent between New York City and Boston had to travel by ship. Often these ships made the long journey to London, England, before the mail was delivered from one city to the next. In the days before telephones, faxes, and the Internet, government officials in New York City and Boston relied on the mail (called the post) for news and official **dispatches**.

King Charles II of England wanted the mail to travel more quickly between the American colonies. He ordered the mail to be sent **overland** from New York City to Boston. At the time, however, a paved road between the cities did not exist. Colonists used Native American trails when they traveled long distances.

King Charles II

To follow the king's order, a man on horseback left New York City on January 22, 1673, with the post in his saddlebags. The **postrider** also carried an ax, which he used to cut his way through parts of the forest.

woodcut of a postrider

On February 5, the postrider arrived in Boston. He delivered mail from the governor of New York to the governor of Massachusetts in Boston. Then he filled his saddlebags with mail from the governor in Boston to take back to New York. It took the postrider another two weeks to make the trip back. This trip was easier, for in places where no tracks existed, the rider could follow paths he had already hacked with his ax.

Later postriders followed this route. Over the years, the road from New York City to Boston grew into three different roads, yet all of them were called the Boston Post Road.

THE BOSTON POST ROAD

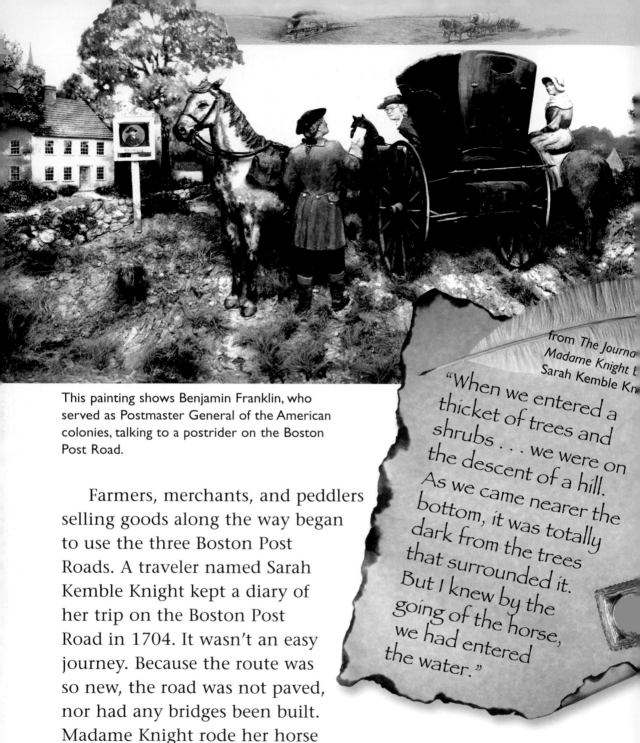

This painting shows Benjamin Franklin, who served as Postmaster General of the American colonies, talking to a postrider on the Boston Post Road.

from The Journal
Madame Knight b
Sarah Kemble Kn

"When we entered a thicket of trees and shrubs . . . we were on the descent of a hill. As we came nearer the bottom, it was totally dark from the trees that surrounded it. But I knew by the going of the horse, we had entered the water."

Farmers, merchants, and peddlers selling goods along the way began to use the three Boston Post Roads. A traveler named Sarah Kemble Knight kept a diary of her trip on the Boston Post Road in 1704. It wasn't an easy journey. Because the route was so new, the road was not paved, nor had any bridges been built. Madame Knight rode her horse through swamps and rivers or had someone take her horse across while she rode in a canoe.

In time, stagecoaches replaced the postriders on horseback. Stagecoaches not only carried the mail, but they also carried passengers from place to place.

Turnpikes were the next **innovation** on the Boston Post Road. A turnpike is a private toll road. People paid to use each stretch of road. These turnpikes went out of business after the railroads came. The idea of the toll road still lives on in modern turnpikes, however.

In the early 1900s, cars and trucks began to travel from New York City to Boston, and to the cities between them. The roads were paved and widened for easier travel. Over time, the Lower Boston Post Road became part of U.S. Route 1. In cities and towns along Route 1, some parts of the road are still named Boston Post Road.

the Boston Post Road as it looks today

9

The Mighty Mississippi

Flowing from north to south, from its **headwaters** in Minnesota all the way to the Gulf of Mexico, the Mississippi River has long been used to carry goods to the ocean. In the 1700s, both Native American and European fur traders traveled on the river in birch bark canoes. Hats made from beaver fur were popular, so traders took beaver **pelts** to a trading post in St. Louis, Missouri, where the Missouri and Mississippi Rivers meet.

a beaver hat

Flat-bottomed boats, or flatboats, then carried the furs down the river to ships waiting at the mouth of the Mississippi. These ships carried the furs on to the East Coast and Europe, where they were made into a variety of fashionable hats.

THE
MISSISSIPPI
RIVER
AND ITS MAJOR
TRIBUTARIES

Scale in Miles
0   100   200   300   400   500

Scale in Kilometers
0   100   200   300 400 500

Water from 40 percent of the nation's rivers drains into the Mississippi River.

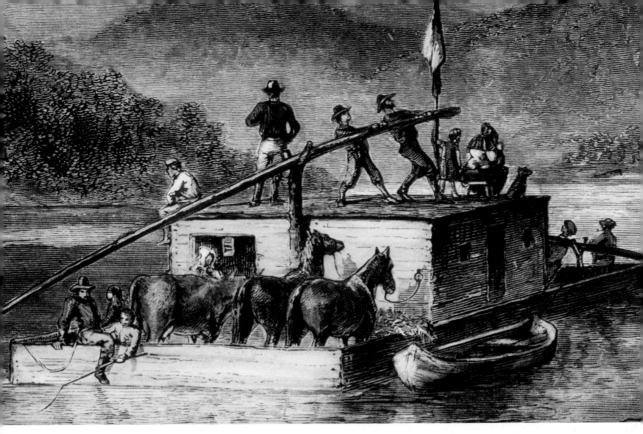

Flatboat crew members used a long pole to steer their way downstream.

When people began wearing silk hats instead of beaver hats, the fur trade dried up. Then, the Mississippi River carried farm goods to market. It cost a farmer in the Ohio Valley less to send his goods down the Ohio and Mississippi Rivers on a flatboat than to have the goods carried over the Appalachian Mountains.

Once the flatboat arrived in the port of New Orleans in Louisiana, the farm goods would be sold and placed on ships to be carried to the East Coast. The boat itself was torn apart and sold for wood. A flatboat's crew could not sail back upstream against the river's strong current. It was not until the steamboat was invented that Mississippi River traffic easily flowed both north and south.

Mississippi River traffic in the 1840s

The *New Orleans* was the first steamboat to travel on the Mississippi. It was on its first voyage in 1811 when an earthquake struck. The Mississippi rolled north, as if the great river were flowing backward—but the *New Orleans* survived the tossing waves. It arrived safely in the city of New Orleans on January 12, 1812.

Steamboats soon traveled up and down the Mississippi, carrying goods and passengers. But when the first railroad bridge crossed the river, it blocked the tall steamboats' way. In 1857, Abraham Lincoln defended the railroad company's right to share the river. Lincoln won, and the steamboat was no longer king of the Mississippi.

Mark Twain

American writer Samuel L. Clemens (1835–1910) grew up in Hannibal, Missouri, on the Mississippi River. He took his pen name, Mark Twain, from the steamboats he worked on. *Mark twain* meant the water was 2 fathoms (12 feet) deep.

In parts of Minnesota, Illinois, and Iowa, waterfalls made the Mississippi River impassable for many years. Canoes could be unloaded and carried over land around the falls, but people could not do this with larger boats.

In the 1930s, the U.S. Army Corps of Engineers built a series of dams and locks on the river from Minneapolis to St. Louis. The locks and dams keep the river 9 feet deep and 400 feet wide, so it is both deep enough and wide enough for river traffic.

Today, once the ice melts in the spring, vessels can travel the length of the river through ten states from Minnesota to Louisiana. Steamboats carry passengers on vacation, whereas towboats and barges carry goods to market.

One towboat usually pushes fifteen barges at once.

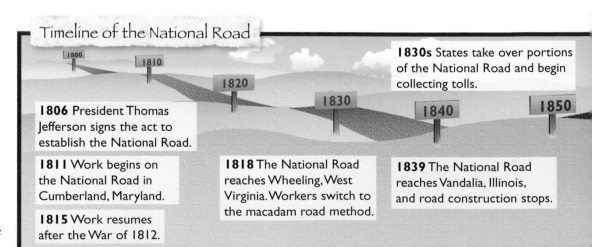

The National Road

After the United States won its independence from England in 1783, the young country stretched from the Atlantic Ocean west to the Mississippi River. Although there were waterways on both sides of this new nation, in the middle sat the Appalachian Mountains. Pittsburgh and Philadelphia were only about 300 miles apart, but mountains separated these two Pennsylvania cities.

The Appalachian Mountains were a major barrier to westward travel.

Goods shipped from Pittsburgh to Philadelphia traveled by water down the Monongahela River to the Ohio River to the Mississippi River to New Orleans. The goods were then loaded on a ship that sailed around the tip of Florida and up the Atlantic Coast to Philadelphia—a trip of more than 3,000 miles!

Timeline of the National Road

1800   1810   1820   1830   1840   1850

1830s States take over portions of the National Road and begin collecting tolls.

1806 President Thomas Jefferson signs the act to establish the National Road.

1811 Work begins on the National Road in Cumberland, Maryland.

1815 Work resumes after the War of 1812.

1818 The National Road reaches Wheeling, West Virginia. Workers switch to the macadam road method.

1839 The National Road reaches Vandalia, Illinois, and road construction stops.

The construction of the National Road involved building many bridges, including this stone bridge in Maryland.

In 1806, President Thomas Jefferson signed an act that called for the creation of a national road. Planners wanted the road to go from east to west, from the waters of the Atlantic Ocean to the Mississippi River.

Work on the road began in Cumberland, Maryland. It followed an earlier Native American trail. Other people, including George Washington, had widened and improved this trail. The first stretch of road was dug and filled with broken rocks. The road was then covered with gravel. Workers received from $12\frac{1}{2}$¢ to $1.00 a day.

After the road reached Wheeling, Virginia (now West Virginia) in 1818, building stopped. Lawmakers couldn't decide how to pay for the next part of the road.

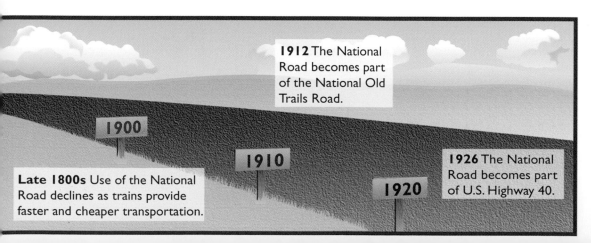

1912 The National Road becomes part of the National Old Trails Road.

1900

1910

1920

1926 The National Road becomes part of U.S. Highway 40.

Late 1800s Use of the National Road declines as trains provide faster and cheaper transportation.

Construction on the National Road began again in 1825 and went on in stages. The road west of Wheeling was built using a new method, the macadam system. Now, the road was built up above ground level, then crushed down with a roller. Named for its inventor, John MacAdam, this new method gave better drainage. The road never reached the Mississippi River. In 1839, it stopped 70 miles short of the river in Vandalia, Illinois. By this time, the railroads were taking **freight** and passengers on faster routes.

Conestoga wagon

Still, the first federal highway was a huge success. Passengers and freight traveled on the National Road. Mail coaches sped along the highway, while farmers walked herds of animals to market. Large Conestoga wagons carried goods both east and west. One wagon could carry 6 to 10 tons of cargo.

John MacAdam's new road-building method raised the roadbed, then compacted the building materials with a roller.

THE TWO STAGES
OF THE
NATIONAL ROAD
1811—1839
—— 1811–1818
—— 1825–1839

By the 1820s, the older parts of the road began to need repairs. The government decided to turn control of the road over to the states through which it passed. They, in turn, began collecting tolls to keep up repairs on the road. Despite this upkeep, the road lost its popularity in the late 1800s. Trains provided a faster and cheaper way to travel.

Cars came next, and cars needed roads to travel on. In 1926, the National Road became part of U.S. Route 40. The road was widened and made into a highway. At one time, Route 40 stretched from coast to coast.

This house was once used to collect tolls along the National Road in Pennsylvania.

After World War II ended in 1945, the federal government decided to create a new highway system across the United States. These new highways were called interstates because they allowed travel between the states. Sections of Route 40 and the National Road were used to create Interstate 70. Parts of the original National Road can still be seen in places.

The Erie Canal

After the National Road was built, people could cross the central part of the Appalachian Mountains. But the road was too far away to help people in the northern states to travel across the mountain ranges.

For years, there had been talk in New York State of creating a waterway to connect the Hudson River to Lake Erie, one of the Great Lakes. This waterway would cross the Catskill range of the Appalachians to link two important New York cities, Albany and Buffalo.

Albany, the state capital, is located in the eastern part of the state on the Hudson River, whereas Buffalo is in western New York on the tip of Lake Erie. The Hudson River flows south to New York City and the Atlantic Ocean. Travelers on the proposed waterway would be able to sail from the Great Lakes all the way to the Atlantic Ocean.

The Mohawk River

Native Americans did have a route west from the Hudson River. Traveling in canoes, they went up the Mohawk River. But travel on this river wasn't practical for large-scale transportation of goods. Waterfalls, rocks, and shallow spots could not be crossed. Boats had to be emptied so that everything could be carried to a better spot.

DeWitt Clinton became governor of New York in 1817. Clinton had seen surveys showing the route the canal would take, and he loved the project. Because the canal would link the Hudson River to Lake Erie, it became known as the Erie Canal.

construction work on the Erie Canal

On July 4, 1817, work began near Rome, New York. Crews began to work on both sides of the city. One crew dug east and the other dug west. Critics called the project "Clinton's Ditch."

Due to **elevation** changes, **locks** had to be built on both sides of this level area. A lock is a water elevator. A lock uses water to raise or lower a boat to the next "floor" of the canal. Once a boat is inside the gate of a lock, the operator adds water to the lock or drains it. When the water level in the lock matches the water level on the other side, the gate is opened.

How a Lock Works

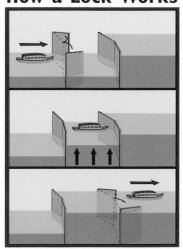

The boat enters the lock and the lower gate is closed.

Water flows into the lock, raising the boat.

When the water level matches the level on the higher side of the lock, the upper gate is opened, and the boat continues on its way.

19

A barge leaves a lock on the Erie Canal in Rome, New York.

Construction on the canal took eight years. Before the canal could reach Buffalo and Lake Erie, it had to pass the town of Lockport. Here, workers blasted through rock to create five locks to raise vessels over a 50-foot cliff and five more locks to lower them again.

On October 26, 1825, the Erie Canal was officially opened. The canal was a great success. It allowed settlers to travel west and goods to travel east. Cities along the canal grew and prospered. Cities farther west also grew, because of the settlers and the business the canal brought them. As DeWitt Clinton had hoped, New York City became the most important port in the United States. The canal paid for itself many times over.

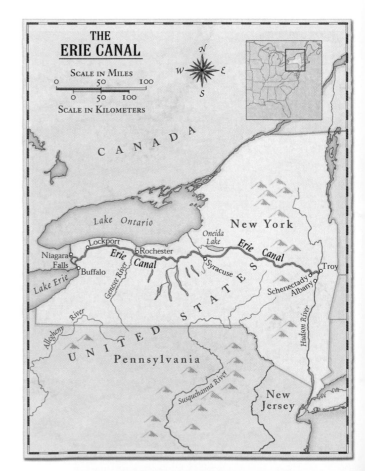

THE ERIE CANAL

SCALE IN MILES
0 50 100

SCALE IN KILOMETERS
0 50 100

The canal lost its passenger business to the railroads, but it was still cheaper to ship goods by barge than by train. The canal was enlarged twice so it could carry more traffic. In 1836, the channels were widened from 40 to 70 feet across. The canal was also deepened from 4 to 7 feet.

In 1905, the Erie Canal was deepened to 14 feet and widened to 200 feet in some places. It was also straightened and joined with three other shorter canals. The new canal was named the New York State Barge Canal.

the Erie Canal

Trucks and planes now can carry freight more quickly than a barge on the canal can. Today, the Erie Canal is used for fun. Towpaths have been made into bike paths. Pleasure boats travel up and down the New York State Canal System.

Low Bridge

On the Erie Canal, every inch of a boat was often filled, so passengers sat on top. When they heard "Low bridge!" the passengers ducked so they would not be knocked off the boat into the water. The phrase was made famous in these words from a song about the canal, written in 1905:

Low bridge, everybody down!
Low bridge, for we're coming through a town!

The Oregon Trail

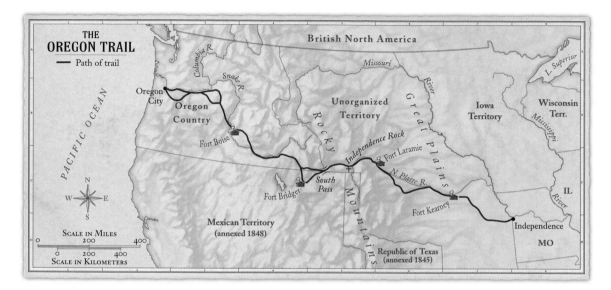

THE
OREGON TRAIL
—— Path of trail

As the country grew, people traveled farther west in search of new land and opportunities. Another set of mountains proved to be a problem: the Rocky Mountains. Native Americans knew a route through the Rockies, but explorers had been frustrated in their efforts to cross the mountain range.

Robert Stuart was the first to discover the South Pass, a 20-mile-wide passage through the Rocky Mountains. Stuart was part of a group of men who had gone to set up a fur-trading post in the Pacific Northwest. The group was on its way back east when the horses were stolen. The men walked through the Rockies until Stuart found an easy way to cross: the South Pass. Twelve years later, another fur trader, Jedediah Smith, rediscovered the South Pass. Members of the Crow nation showed him the wide, flat passage.

After these early discoveries of the South Pass became known, fur traders created a trail. It started in Missouri and ended 2,000 miles farther away in Oregon. Every spring, traders who worked for the American Fur Company followed this trail to carry supplies to the company's station in Oregon Country, as it was known.

In 1835, Dr. Marcus Whitman traveled to Oregon with the fur company's wagon train. He decided to settle in Oregon. The following year Whitman married. He took his wife over the trail to Oregon.

In the years that followed, other settlers went to Oregon over the trail in search of land. Word of Oregon's fertile soil and plentiful timber reached people back in the eastern states. In 1843, the "great **migration**" began. That year, almost a thousand wagons traveled in a long line called a wagon train over the Oregon Trail.

Oregon Country

Before 1846, both the United States and Great Britain claimed "Oregon Country." Some settlers felt they were being patriotic to the United States by helping to settle the land. Then in 1846, a treaty established that the land belonged to the United States. Oregon became a U.S. territory in 1848 and became a state in 1859.

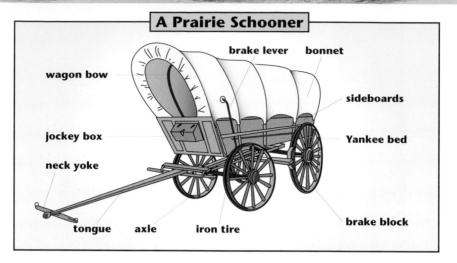

A Prairie Schooner

wagon bow
brake lever
bonnet
sideboards
jockey box
Yankee bed
neck yoke
tongue
axle
iron tire
brake block

The typical wagon that crossed the Oregon Trail was called a prairie schooner. These schooners were smaller than the Conestoga wagons that traveled over the National Road. Pulling a heavy wagon in the mountains was too difficult for oxen and horses.

Much of the Oregon Trail followed rivers because both people and animals needed water to drink. The trail followed the Platte River across the prairie. In the foothills of the Rockies, the trail followed the Sweetwater River to Independence Rock. Many pioneers carved their names on this large rock, where some signatures can still be seen today. The river led them on to the South Pass, still the easiest way to cross the steep Rocky Mountains.

Independence Rock

On the Oregon Trail, Sallie Hester, age fourteen, wrote: "Passed Independence Rock. This rock is covered with names. With great difficulty I found a place to cut mine."

John Livingston

Oregon offered opportunities to many people, including John Livingston, a childhood friend of Samuel Clemens. Born into slavery, Livingston was freed during the Civil War and arrived in Oregon in 1864. He worked at various jobs and owned 180 acres of land at the time of his death in 1912.

Once the travelers reached the top of the Rocky Mountains, they also reached the **Continental Divide**. The rivers on each side of this ridge of mountains flow in opposite directions. After crossing the divide, travelers on the Oregon Trail followed rivers west to Fort Hall. There, the wagon trains divided. Some went south to California. Others followed the Snake River to Oregon.

Travelers bound for Oregon still had to cross the Blue Mountains and the rapids on the Columbia River. If they didn't make it in time, the winter snows would delay their trip by months.

Ruts made by wagon wheels can still be seen on parts of the Oregon National Historic Trail.

From 1843 to 1869, thousands of settlers and **prospectors** traveled west every year on the Oregon Trail. When the railroads went west, however, travel on the trail slowed and then stopped. Why walk for five months to reach Oregon if you could ride there in days? Today, tourists hike and drive on the Oregon National Historic Trail and remember the longest wagon trail in history.

The Transcontinental Railroad

a painting of the *Best Friend of Charleston*

The first steam locomotive to carry passengers in the United States was called the *Best Friend of Charleston*. It started in South Carolina in 1830 and ran along 6 miles of track. After this time, the number of railroads in the United States grew quickly. Trains were faster than stagecoaches or boats. People began to think about using a train to travel across the entire country.

In 1845, a businessman from New York asked Congress to give him land to build a railroad across the continent. The government said no. They didn't think it was possible. But so many people used the Oregon Trail to travel west in the 1840s that the idea of a **transcontinental** railroad began to seem more practical. In 1853, Congress sent crews out to study possible routes.

After many years of discussion, Congress finally agreed to build a railroad line that would reach California. In 1862, President Abraham Lincoln signed the Pacific Railroad Act. Two railroad companies would build the new line. The Union Pacific would start in Omaha, Nebraska, and go west. The Central Pacific would start in Sacramento, California, and go east.

Both railroads faced problems. The Central Pacific Railroad had to cross the Sierra Nevada Mountains. Workers had to dig or blast parts of the mountain away to make room for the tracks.

Workers on the Transcontinental Railroad had to blast their way through the Sierra Nevada Mountains.

27

The Central Pacific had another problem: a shortage of labor. The construction chief convinced the company to try Chinese workers. Many Chinese people had immigrated to California in the early 1800s.

The Chinese workers quickly impressed the railroad managers. They dug up ground, drove spikes, put down tracks, and dynamited mountain slopes. Thousands of Chinese workers would help to build the Transcontinental Railroad.

Many Civil War **veterans** worked for the Union Pacific Railroad. They built the railroad across miles of treeless prairies. The wood they needed for the railroad ties had to be sent from other places.

The two railroads met at last in Promontory Point, Utah. Officials from both railroads went to see the final spike driven into the rails. On May 10, 1869, a special spike made of gold was driven into the last railroad tie. The completed track was 1,776 miles long.

Route of the Transcontinental Railroad

Promontory, UT

Omaha, NE

Sacramento, CA

Areas served by railroads by 1850
Union Pacific
Central Pacific

Chinese workers played a major part in building the Central Pacific Railroad.

a copy of the historic golden spike

By order of the government, the railroads had installed telegraph lines along the new track. A telegraph wire was attached to the hammer that hit the special spike. As the hammer struck the spike, the wire sent a signal across the country using Morse Code. The United States was united at last!

Days after the ceremony, the railroad line began service. Passengers could travel from Sacramento, California, to Omaha, Nebraska, in days, not months. By connecting to other rail lines, travelers could go from the Atlantic to the Pacific!

Trade and travel between east and west increased. People and goods traveled quickly from one side of the country to the other. These rail lines are still used today.

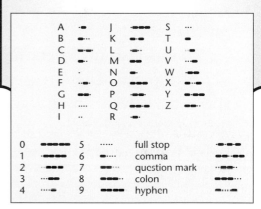

Morse Code

Tap a telegraph, and it sends electricity on the line. A short tap is called a dot and a long tap is called a dash. The inventor of the telegraph, Samuel Morse, created a code that uses dots and dashes to spell words or numbers.

A	J	S
B	K	T
C	L	U
D	M	V
E	N	W
F	O	X
G	P	Y
H	Q	Z
I	R	

0	5	full stop
1	6	comma
2	7	question mark
3	8	colon
4	9	hyphen

East meets west at Promontory Point.

Conclusion

Routes develop as a way of meeting people's needs. Sometimes business drives the need. The Boston Post Road and the Erie Canal developed so that mail and goods could be moved from place to place.

The Mississippi River always existed as a route. However, the Army Corps of Engineers improved the river by adding locks so that goods could be shipped more easily.

Routes also take people from place to place. The Oregon Trail shows that when many people desperately want to get from one place to another, they will carve out a way.

To meet people's needs, new roads are built and old ones are improved or changed.

Some routes are developed to meet both needs. The National Road was built so that people and goods could travel from one side of the country to the other. When the country grew even larger, the Transcontinental Railroad answered these needs.

People continue to develop new routes today. Look for the orange cones and construction signs along highways, and you can see routes change right before your eyes!

Glossary

continent	one of the principal land masses of Earth
Continental Divide	the high point of a continent where rivers flow in opposite directions
dispatches	official reports, usually sent quickly
elevation	height above the level of the sea
freight	goods carried by a vehicle or vessel
headwaters	the source of a body of water
innovation	new idea
locks	enclosed water elevators with gates at each end, used to raise or lower boats so they can pass through areas at different elevations
migration	the movement of a group of people from one place to another
overland	going over land
pelts	animal skins with their fur
postrider	person who rides on a post road to carry the mail
prospectors	people who explore a region for minerals and precious metals
transcontinental	extending or going across a continent
turnpikes	toll roads, requiring payment for travel
veterans	people who have served in the armed forces

Index

Appalachian Mountains 11, 14, 18

Army Corps of Engineers 13, 30

Atlantic Ocean 14–15, 18

Boston Post Road 6–9, 30

Charles II, King of England 6

Clemens, Samuel L. (Mark Twain)
  12, 25

Clinton, DeWitt 19–20

Conestoga Wagon 16, 24

Crow nation 22

Erie Canal 18–21, 30

Franklin, Benjamin 8

Hester, Sallie 24

Independence Rock 24

Jefferson, Thomas 14, 15

Knight, Sarah Kemble 8

Lincoln, Abraham 12, 27

Livingston, John 25

MacAdam, John 16

Mississippi River 10–13, 14–16, 30

Morse, Samuel 29

Morse Code 29

National Road 14–17, 24, 30

Native Americans 5, 6, 10, 15,
  18, 22

Oregon Trail 22–25, 26, 30

prairie schooner 24

railroad 9, 12, 16, 21, 25, 26–29

Rocky Mountains 22–25

Smith, Jedediah 22

South Pass 22–24

stagecoach 9, 26

Stuart, Robert 22

Transcontinental Railroad 26–29,
  30

Twain, Mark (Samuel L. Clemens)
  12

Vespucci, Amerigo 4

Washington, George 15

Whitman, Marcus 23